Little Lamb Finds Christmas

Written by Cathy Gilmore
Illustrated by Kim Wilson

This book is dedicated to all the catechists and children
who are taught by the loving hand of the Holy Spirit
through the Catechesis of the Good Shepherd
who have inspired me so much.

–Cathy

Imprimi Potest:
Harry Grile, CSsR, Provincial
Denver Province, The Redemptorists

Published by Liguori Publications
Liguori, Missouri 63057

To order, visit Liguori.org or call 800-325-9521

p ISBN 978-0-7648-2489-0
e ISBN 978-0-7648-6970-9

Liguori Publications, a nonprofit corporation, is an apostolate of The Redemptorists. To learn more about The Redemptorists, visit Redemptorists.com.

Printed in China
18 17 16 15 14 / 5 4 3 2 1
First Edition

My name is _____.

The Good Shepherd knows my name, and I belong to him.

Jesus, please bless _____ , who gave me this book on _____.

Hi! I'm *Lemi*,
and I love Christmas!

Do you want to know why?
It's quite a story....

4

It started one wintry day.
My shepherd (I call him **Sha**-*baa*)
led the flock to a pasture
on the hills near Bethlehem.

6

Most lambs are good at following,
but I was always getting lost.
Little by little, bit by bit,
I nibbled myself away from the others.

I slipped into a thicket.
"**Baa-hoo**," I whimpered.

My fleece tangled in some thorns.
I was *stuck*.

Sha-baa left the rest, almost a hundred sheep,
to come and find me.
"Ah, there you are!" he sighed.

He reached down, untangled me,
and carried me back to the flock,
cheering, "I found my lost lamb!"

At bedtime, we rested under a big, starry sky.
It was a cold night. We huddled together.
Even Sha-baa slept with us.

Suddenly, the night was filled with light and music!
Angels appeared, and they spoke to Sha-baa!

Tonight a Savior and King is born.

Find the Child lying in a manger.

I knew about mangers.
Mangers were boxes filled with food.
Babies do *not* sleep in mangers—
especially baby kings!

Was the baby *lost*?
If anyone could find him,
Sha-baa could—I knew it!

15

Sha-baa grabbed his staff and ran down the hill toward Bethlehem.
I wanted to see the manger baby, too!
I trotted behind Sha-baa.
He didn't see me. He didn't hear me.
I couldn't keep up.
I was lost...*again.*

What could I do?
A bright star glowed
over a cave at the edge of town.
Maybe Sha-baa went there.
I followed the light.

18

I heard a noise.
A shadow moved.
A LION—right behind me!
Was he following the light
or looking for a snack?
I wasn't taking any chances.

I bolted toward the cave.
"Whoa, little lamb!" some
shepherds said with a laugh.
I found Sha-baa!
Relieved, I panted:
"Baa, haa, haa,,,,"

20

Sha-baa held me and pointed.
"Shh!" he whispered.

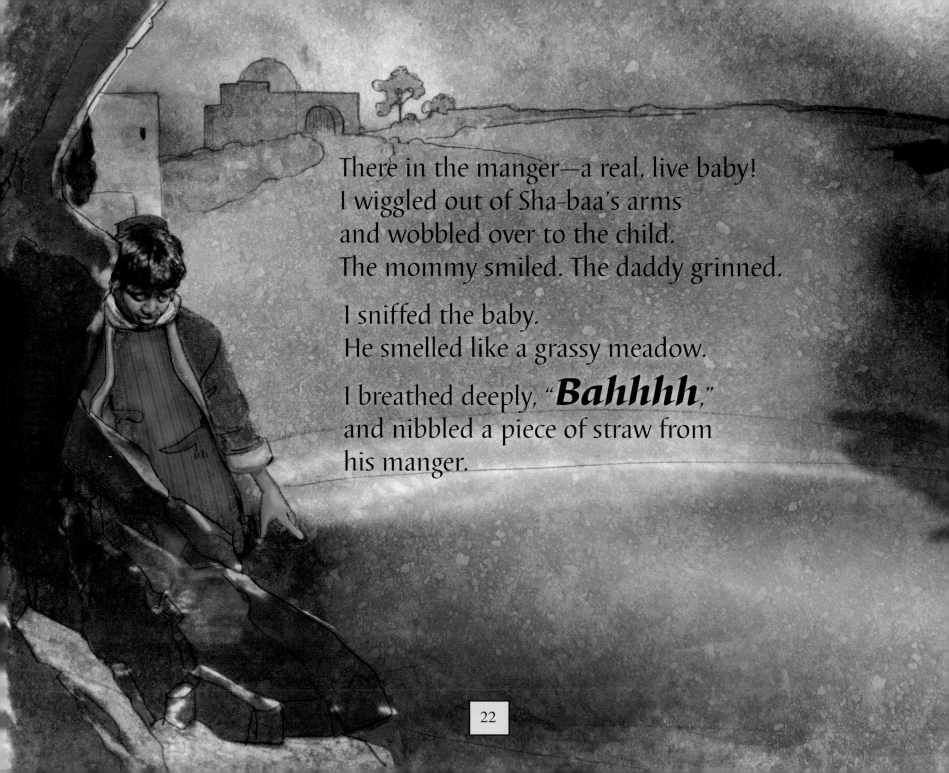

There in the manger—a real, live baby!
I wiggled out of Sha-baa's arms
and wobbled over to the child.
The mommy smiled. The daddy grinned.

I sniffed the baby.
He smelled like a grassy meadow.

I breathed deeply, "**_Bahhhh_**,"
and nibbled a piece of straw from
his manger.

Usually, sheep and shepherds don't visit
newborn babies.
We smell bad.
We hardly ever take baths.
But this family was different.
They offered each shepherd a
chance to *hold* the baby.

I bleated a soft hello to the little king.
The baby *smiled* at me.
Each curl of my fleece felt soft and safe.

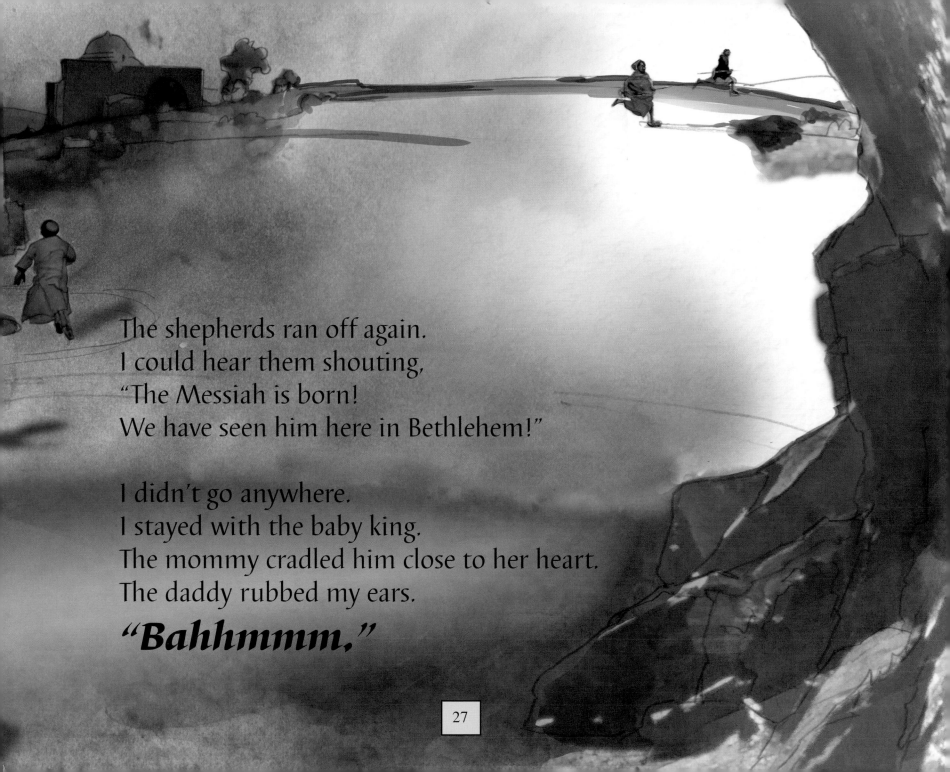

The shepherds ran off again.
I could hear them shouting,
"The Messiah is born!
We have seen him here in Bethlehem!"

I didn't go anywhere.
I stayed with the baby king.
The mommy cradled him close to her heart.
The daddy rubbed my ears.
"Bahhmmm,"

"God's Son has another visitor," he said.
I looked outside.

"Baaaak!" I blurted loudly and fiercely.
The visitor was...the...the lion!
He had followed me!

29

Slowly the lion crept near.
I jumped from the daddy's arms
and stood between the lion and the baby.
I trembled only a little.

Now the lion seemed to smile.
He crouched down and *bowed*
before the baby king.
The daddy stroked the lion's fur.
"Don't be afraid. He means us no harm."

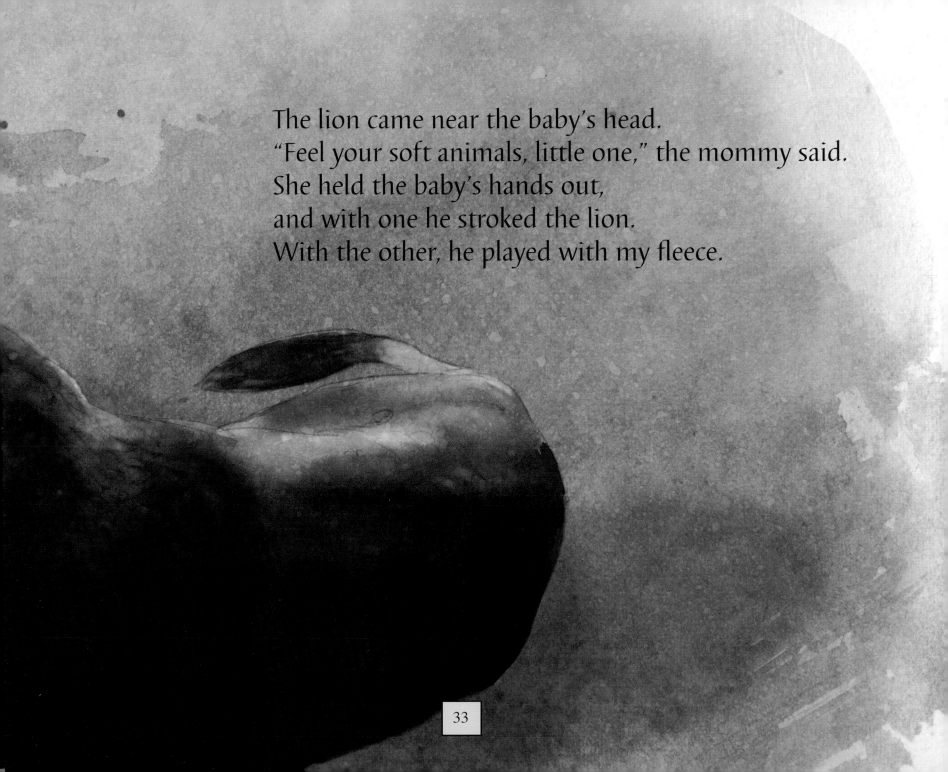

The lion came near the baby's head.
"Feel your soft animals, little one," the mommy said.
She held the baby's hands out,
and with one he stroked the lion.
With the other, he played with my fleece.

She said,
"Strong lion, gentle lamb, meet my Son,
God's promise and gift, for whom all creation has waited.
Though tiny, he is your Shepherd and King.
In his kingdom,
the hurt are healed,
the lost are found,
and lions and lambs live together in peace."

The lion nodded, nuzzled my head,
and strode into the dark.
What a glorious night!

35

See why I love Christmas?
I found my forever shepherd—
I belong to a king!
Even when I'm alone, I'm never lost,
because he watches over me. I am his special little lamb.

Thank you, Jesus, for Christmas, and for loving little lambs like me!

A *Lion* in Bethlehem?

In the first century, lions still roamed the countryside of Israel. These lions are known as Persian, Asiatic, or Indian lions: They are smaller, with darker, thicker fur than their African cousins. Lions were both feared and admired

in the part of the world where Jesus was born. In those days, lions were often used in art as symbols of power, kingship, and courage. The Bible is full of lion imagery. Jesus himself, as the Messiah foreshadowed by the prophets, was called "the lion of the tribe of Judah" (Revelation 5:5, see also Genesis 49:9–10).

It was not so rare for a brave shepherd to occasionally contend with a lion in protecting his flock. In 1 Samuel 17:34–36, David, still a shepherd boy from Bethlehem, tells King Saul how he had to defend his sheep from a lion.

Throughout history, there are many stories of animals who show uncanny instinctive responses of worship (bowing, following, etc.) upon encountering a sacred presence. You may even imagine that a lion could have been the first "king" to bow before the Messiah.

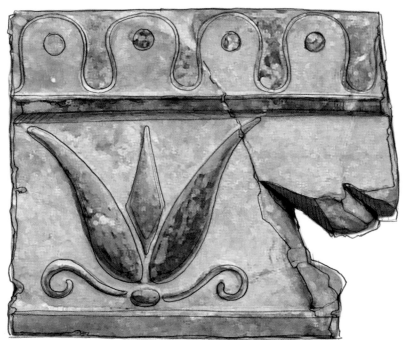

It's nice to remember that Jesus not only loves lambs, but lions, too. In God's kingdom, there are no predators or prey. Truly, Jesus is the Prince of Peace.

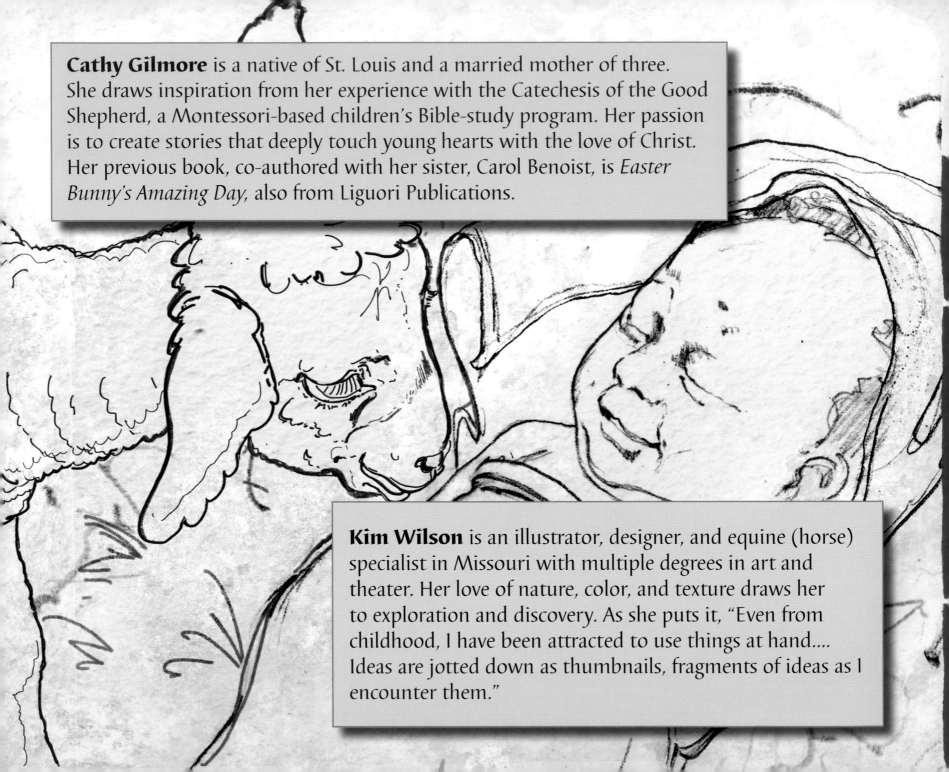

Cathy Gilmore is a native of St. Louis and a married mother of three. She draws inspiration from her experience with the Catechesis of the Good Shepherd, a Montessori-based children's Bible-study program. Her passion is to create stories that deeply touch young hearts with the love of Christ. Her previous book, co-authored with her sister, Carol Benoist, is *Easter Bunny's Amazing Day,* also from Liguori Publications.

Kim Wilson is an illustrator, designer, and equine (horse) specialist in Missouri with multiple degrees in art and theater. Her love of nature, color, and texture draws her to exploration and discovery. As she puts it, "Even from childhood, I have been attracted to use things at hand.... Ideas are jotted down as thumbnails, fragments of ideas as I encounter them."